World of Farming

Seasons on a Farm

Nancy Dickmann

Heinemann Library
Chicago, Illinois

www.heinemannraintree.com
Visit our website to find out more information about Heinemann-Raintree books.

To order:
☎ Phone 888-454-2279

💻 Visit www.heinemannraintree.com to browse our catalog and order online.

Edited by Siân Smith, Nancy Dickmann, and Rebecca Rissman
Designed by Joanna Hinton-Malivoire
Picture research by Mica Brancic
Production by Victoria Fitzgerald
Originated by Capstone Global Library Ltd
Printed and bound in China by South China Printing Company Ltd

ISBN 978 1 4329 3939 7
15 14 13 12 11 10
10 9 8 7 6 5 4 3 2

Library of Congress Cataloging-in-Publication Data
Dickmann, Nancy.
  Seasons on a farm / Nancy Dickmann.—1st ed.
    p. cm.—(World of farming)
  Includes bibliographical references and index.
  ISBN 978-1-4329-3939-7 (hc)—ISBN 978-1-4329-3953-3 (pb)
1. Seasons—Juvenile literature. 2. Farm life—Juvenile literature. 3. Farms—Juvenile literature. I. Title. II. Series: Dickmann, Nancy. World of farming.
  QB637.4.D53 2010
  630—dc22
                                    2009051588

Acknowledgements
We would like to thank the following for permission to reproduce photographs: Corbis pp.**7** (© Image Source), **17** (zefa Select/© Awilli), **22** (zefa Select/© Awilli); Getty Images pp.**18** (Comstock/Jupiter Images), **20**, **23 bottom** (Dorling Kindersley/Alan Buckingham); Photolibrary pp.**4** (Digital Light Source/Sergio Izquierdo), **5** (imagebroker.net/Michael Krabs), **6** (Britain On View/Chris Laurens), **8** (Reso/Diaphor La Phototheque), **9** (F1Online RF/Sodapix Sodapix), **10** (Robert Harding Travel/Ann & Steve Toon), **11** (Juniors Bildarchiv), **12** (Index Stock Imagery/Inga Spence), **13** (Neil Duncan), **14** (Tips Italia/Bildagentur RM), **15** (age fotostock/Alan Kearney), **16** (Digital Light Source/Richard Hutchings), **19** (Nordic Photos/Mikael Andersson), **21, 23 middle** (All Canada Photos/Don Weixl), **23 top** (Britain On View/Chris Laurens).

Front cover photograph of strawberries being harvested reproduced with permission of Shutterstock (© Boris Khamitsevich). Back cover photograph of a ewe with lamb in Scotland reproduced with permission of Photolibrary (Robert Harding Travel/Ann & Steve Toon).

The publisher would like to thank Dee Reid, Diana Bentley, and Nancy Harris for their invaluable help with this book.

Every effort has been made to contact copyright holders of material reproduced in this book. Any omissions will be rectified in subsequent printings if notice is given to the publishers.

Contents

What Is a Farm?

sweet corn

A farm is a place where food is grown.

Farms change with the seasons.

Spring

plow

In spring, farmers plow the fields.

They get fields ready for planting.

In spring, farmers plant seeds.

The seeds will grow into plants.

In spring, lambs are born.

Calves are born in spring, too.

Summer

In summer, plants grow taller.

Farmers water their plants.

Fall

In fall, plants are ready to be picked.

Some farmers gather wheat.

In fall, some farmers pick apples.

hay

Some farmers make hay to feed their animals.

Winter

In winter, farmers fix their
farm machines.

Farmers make sure their animals stay warm.

seeds

In winter, farmers buy seeds to plant in spring.

The farm gets ready for spring.

Can You Remember?

What do farmers make hay for?

22

Answer on page 24

Picture Glossary

 **plow** farm tool that breaks up the ground so that farmers can plant seeds

 **season** a time of the year. Spring, summer, fall, and winter are seasons.

 **seed** plants grow from seeds. Farmers plant seeds in the ground.

Index

Answer to quiz on page 22: Farmers make hay so that they can feed it to their animals.

Note to Parents and Teachers

Before reading:
Ask the children to name the four seasons. Then look at a calendar together to agree when these seasons take place. What is the weather like during the different seasons?

After reading:
- As a class, make a circular picture of the seasons on a farm. Divide a large circle of paper into quarters and split the class into four groups. Give each group a season and ask them to draw pictures of what happens on the farm during that season. Have them cut out the pictures and stick them on their quarter of the circle. Then display the finished picture on the classroom wall.

- Talk about when the fruits and vegetables that grow where you live are ready to eat. Make a frieze showing each month of the year and look at books and the Internet together to find out when local foods are ready to harvest. Have the children draw these fruits and vegetables and stick them on the correct month. Talk about how some foods can be stored so we can eat them during winter.